Reflective Contemplations

A Tribute to Life

Lorna Ramirez

Published in Australia by Lorna Ramirez
First published in Australia February 2018
This edition published 2018
Copyright © Lorna Ramirez 2018
Cover design, typesetting: Chameleon Print Design

The right of Lorna Ramirez to be identified as the Author of the Work has been asserted in accordance with the Copyright, Designs and Patents Act 1988.

All rights reserved. No part of this publication may be reproduced, stored in a retrieval system, or transmitted, in any form or by any means without the prior written permission of the publisher, nor be otherwise circulated in any form of binding or cover other than that in which it is published and without a similar condition being imposed on the subsequent purchaser.

Ramirez, Lorna
Reflective Contemplations: A Tribute to Life
ISBN: 978-0-6482130-2-4
pp126

About the Author

Lorna Ramirez was born, raised and educated in Manila in the Philippines, attaining a degree in chemical engineering and working as a laboratory manager in a textiles company.

In 1977, with her husband and her son and daughter, she migrated to Australia. She worked as a laboratory technician and a chemist in Australia, only retiring in the year 2000 to care for her first grandchild.

Lorna Ramirez has travelled extensively, gaining much from her interactions with people all over the world and building a strong foundation for her philosophies about life. She loves gardening, cooking and reading and playing the piano. She is also interested in the stock exchange.

She has published three books: *My Innermost Thoughts* in 2014 and *My Passion, My Calling* in 2015 and *Moments of Love, Lust and Ecstasy* in 2017. She won third prize for the 2017 Christmas Writing Competition by the Society of Women Writers of Victoria. In October 2016 Lorna was one of the recipients of a certificate of recognition from FILCCA (Filipino Community Council of Australia).

Lorna is also a regular contributor for *The Philippine Times* in Melbourne and *The Philippine Sentinel* in Sydney. Throughout her life Lorna Ramirez, a woman of faith, has been a wise observer of human behaviour and has collected her many wisdoms and observations to produce this inspiring and uplifting book.

Acknowledgements

Special Thanks to Alyssa Cary
my Personal Assistant

Dedicated To

My loving husband, Claro

Grandchildren Alyssa and Amelia

Children and their partners:

Carlo and Marie

Maria and Steve

My sister Victoria Polon

Preface

This book is a collection of articles I had written and were published at *The Philippine Times* Melbourne newspaper. The book also included my original written poems, inspirational messages and quotes. Any similarities to other writings are purely coincidental.

My love and close bonding with my families, loved ones and friends and my strong connection with GOD had inspired me to write all the beautiful passages and inspirational messages'

I believe as we mature our perspective and priorities in life will change, hence I am happy to share to all people; my life experiences, knowledge gained, lessons learned, my convictions and the philosophies I had developed throughout my life

I hope that the readers will enjoy as well as relate to the topics and sensitive issues that were presented in this book *Reflective Contemplations*.

—By Lorna Ramirez

A. Contemplations

1
A Tribute To Life

Waking up each day is a celebration of life. A life of new beginning. To be able to cherish once again, and enjoy life itself. It becomes routine and normal for all of us to wake up each day and we have taken it for granted. Then one day we learn that there are those who are not given a chance to do it all again. Instead they have succumbed to deep slumber, the pangs of death came and the bereft of life has been taken away from them. Leaving loved ones, families and friends in pain and sorrows. Let's appreciate each day, waking up thankful that we are still here, enjoying the breath of life… Let's pray for those who were not given a chance to do so.

I vividly remember, during my university years I had a close friend. She was pretty, smart, and belonged to a wealthy family. She was very popular in our engineering campus, and being an only child she had everything in life. On our final exam there was shocking news, she had died in her sleep. We were all devastated.

This experience made me see life from a different perspective. Treasuring and enjoying each moment shared with families and friends. Before and after waking up acknowledging and thanking God for all the blessings received for the day. I always say "I love you" to my loved ones, because I do not know if there will be a chance for me to say it tomorrow. Each day I try to do things that I am passionate about such as tickling the ivory keys, writing, gardening, and appreciating everything that I have. At times we should try to help others, especially those who need it the most. But there will be instances where you will get frustrated and upset when you are generous and people will try to take advantage of you, one ugly side of human nature. Indeed we do all have our weaknesses and imperfections. However being aware of it and trying to overcome it is much better than doing nothing at all.

As the popular saying goes, "life is too short to be miserable," so let's live life to the fullest. Don't let envy, greed, and jealousy reign to our hearts, and in failing to do so you will not find inner peace within yourself and your fellowmen.

An excerpt from my book,
My Innermost Thoughts

We should never pass the day
Without giving thanks
For our blessings,
Each day is a challenge we have to face
Each day is another day on which
We will be able to build
Our dreams and foundations
For a better tomorrow.
Don't let it be wasted.

1 A Tribute To Life

2
A Tribute to all Mothers

To be a mother is the noblest job of all, but the most underrated. It is the very reason why it should always be celebrated each year. It is an acknowledgment of all the hard work, sacrifices, juggling the time for those who are working, just to have and share quality and precious time with their family.

Being a mother myself, I still worry for my children no matter how old they are. Now that they have children of their own, my role as a mother never ends. The work continues, giving the love and care to the grandchildren.

A mother's heart is so strong, it can withstand the pain inflicted by loved ones, or even by their own children. A mother's love is a selfless love that keeps on forgiving and giving, until there is no more left for them to give.

A mother's love is so understanding and supportive, guiding their children in every possible way. However at times, children can go astray, the influence of friends and environments can be stronger than the care and love we give them. I feel the pain of the parents going through this.

Indeed, mother's love is lasting, endless, unconditional, and beyond comprehension. No one can fathom what a mother's love is, unless you are a mother.

Excerpt from
My Passion My Calling:

It is the mother's heart
That children can find
Assurance of being loved
It is in the mother's arms
That children can find solace
And comfort, but
It is in the mother's hugs and kisses
That they can find the real joy
Of being loved and most of all
Being special and cared for

3
Father's of Today

Arguably fathers are the wind beneath the wings of family units and of institutions; a protector, defender, bread winner, and the guiding light. Yes, things have changed. It is the evolution of the new fathers of today in contrast to the far cry from the old years where household work and looking after children was solely the responsibilities of mothers.

I grew up in a family with my father as the bread winner and my mother who stayed at home to care for us. However, my parents broke the hold of gender roles and encouraged us to pursue university degrees in order to have a better and more successful future.

With more and more women in the workforce pursuing their careers and ambitions, there is no alternative but for a husband to actively do a fair share of household work, especially in countries like Australia where domestic help is uncommon and child care services are too expensive.

Because of the present insecurities of today such as redundancies, layoffs, factory closures, and dependence on the incomes of mothers, some fathers decide to be stay at home dads which was an unthinkable situation in my time. Whatever happened to the "Male ego"? I believe that couples at present are being practical and sensible in their endeavours that are unsolicited by forced gender roles. And why not?

The family and looking after the children are the most important thing in the world.

With the advocacy of equal rights, we are seeing more and more husbands looking after the children and the home. When I was baby-sitting my grandchildren and attending a mother's group, some who were actively involved were fathers and their children; a beautiful scene to watch and witness. Hence the evolution of what fathers of today are.

In this modern era some families consist of two fathers or two mothers and society accepts this as a normal way of life.

Being a father is not an easy job. Fathers have tried to be strong, but deep within they do have a soft spot for their children. In some difficult and crucial situations fathers remain calm and strong, as their children continue to look up to and idolise them.

No matter what the situations in today's technological world, a father's heart and soul never changes. He loves his family to a point that he will protect them to his last breath of life.

Fathers are disciplinarians, yet they are caring, affectionate and loving. In turn children will look for partners who resemble their parents, and will take after the characteristics of their parents, their role models form childhood. Fathers especially have a great influence and important role in their families.

We should give credit and acknowledgement to single fathers who act the roles of both parents. The sacrifices that he will do to be able to achieve a healthy and happy life for his children and beyond compare.

Suffice to say that it is paramount and relevant to celebrate father's day, not only during this month of September but all year round to give fathers the recognition of the sacrifices and their active involvement in moulding their children to be the best of what they can be.

Needless to say, fathers make the life in family institution rewarding and worth living.

>Excerpt from my book
>*My Passion My Calling*
>
>'To a husband'
>Through the years pass
>The stronger bond still exists
>Both of us had changed physically
>But we have grown stronger together
>With a more mature outlook in life
>Thus the love for one another
>Continues to flow
>Regardless of all obstacles
>We have endured
>As we walk through our journry
>Of our lives
>Proud to have him as my husband
>My soulmate and my real
>Best Friend

3 Father's of Today

4
Acceptance Versus Tolerance

Acceptance and tolerance are two words that majority of people do not know the difference. The truth is they are world apart. Acceptance is the higher level of tolerance. Tolerance means you can tolerate something but not necessarily accepting it.

In the modern era, most of us will show tolerance to sensitive issues such as race, religion and most especially to the LGBT (Lesbian, Gay, Bisexual and Transgendered), but are they widely accepted by the majority of the population?

At the early century in medieval Europe, homosexuality was considered a sodomy even punishable by death. Even today they were called names such as queer, gay, faggot etc. At times families disown their own offspring because of this issue.

In 1980's the gay community had a setback. They were antagonised because of the Aid's epidemic. A big blow to them. Through the years with more and more celebrities and entertainers coming out of their closets plus the role of the media had helped significantly the war against homophobic.

Indeed Homosexual (LGBT) had gone a long way since the early centuries and even in the early 20th century. Is it because we are more educated now and the influence of social media changed the way people think or are we just became more rational, open minded and people nowadays are not conservative and religious than before?

that we are all different and loving someone with the same gender does not mean their love is inferior than those who love the opposite sex. I do believe that a person will be the one to decide who they really are and not to be dictated and pressured by the society. Their mind, heart and soul will decide what gender they are comfortable with. Regardless of what they chose (choose) they deserve to be happy.

What will be your reaction if one of your children will inform you that they are different? It will be frustrating of course, but there is nothing much we can do, we should support them. Its not their fault it is just unfortunate they were born in a wrong body.

It is quite timely that this issue is in my latest book, Moments of Love, Lust and Ecstasy. I never expected it to be an issue this year in Australia.

Very interesting to see the result of the poll about the same sex marriage. Whatever the result will be, we should respect the decision of the majority. If it is a yes vote perhaps its time for us to reflect and embrace the word acceptance, anyway that is what the world needs now!

Excerpts from my book
My Innermost Thoughts

Acceptance

Its easy to love the lovable
Its easy to accept people
Who share our beliefs and convictions
Its easy to love families and friends
It will take courage for us
To love and accept people
Who are different unlovable
This would be a peaceful place
If we tried to accept and respect everyone
Regardless of gender race or religion
And other differences

4 *Acceptance Versus Tolerance*

5
Fear of the Unknown

Excerpt from my Book
My Innermost Thoughts

Fear of the unknown is one
Of the reasons we are reluctant
To do things out of our comfort zone
But once we decided to take risk
And have succeeded
The benefits are endless
Then we will never look back
However for those who have failed
At least we can learn from our mistakes
Thus inspiring us to do better next time around

In today's environment, we are witnessing terrorism attacks in public places, concerts, the random unreasonable shootings in public places, schools, our fear of the unknown is at the highest level. Its so sad if we succumb to this. We will become prisoners of ourselves and the fear will deter us from enjoying our lives.

Fear of the unknown is akin to the fear of doing things out of our comfort zone. The fear of failure is always in our mind. Successful people take risk, but with calculated risk. They do have alternative plan if things did not work out. They managed to assess and learn from their mistakes that gave them motivation to do it all over again till they succeeded.

Lack of knowledge is also a contributing factor for our fear of the unknown and most often the fear is unsubstantiated hence preventing them to experiment, take risk and progress will never be achieved.

Childhood tragedy, traumatic experiences and unhappy childhood are also amongst the reasons for our fear of the unknown. They would prefer to be on the safe side, scared of changes, and prefer a stable and constant surroundings.

Fear of the unknown will deter us to tap our outmost potential. We won't be able to explore our hidden talents. We should always remember that life itself is a gamble and venturing into different avenues in life are at times worth fulfilling and satisfying and definitely one of the recipes for success.

Indeed, there are ways to overcome your fear. First and foremost is to analyse and comprehend your fear. Do research and gather facts. The worst thing is doing nothing and not knowing if it is worth a try, thus missing opportunities and the failure of the realisation of your dreams to come true. Another one is by doing it slowly facing your fear one step at a time till you conquer your fear. You can also read inspiring books, talk to people, ask for the support of your families and friends.

Year 1977 when we decided to migrate to Australia. We had our doubts. Both of us had a good paying job, financially stable, but we chose to migrate. Going to a country with no families and friends and with young children was a gamble. We had overcome our fear and we never looked back. The best decision we had.

Regardless of how old you are, you can still face your fear. Learn new things, be adventurous after all, life is too short to be doing nothing!

6
Dad...The Hero

Most of us are fascinated with *super heroes*. Children always have their favourite super hero but their real living super heroes through their eyes are their Dads.

The sons perceive their father as an idol, wishing to be like him when they grow up. The daughters when they were young view their fathers as their knights in shining armours ready to help and protect them from everything.

Not all fathers are worthy being good fathers, but generally fathers always love, care and are the ultimate protectors of the families, hence they are the strength of a family institution.

Dads are always fun to be with. They play soccer, football and other sports with their children. A father will be there for his family, he is expected to be responsible and carry the weight on all the problems of the family and of course with the help of his wife.

The interactions of the children with fathers during early childhood will develop the children personalities in their adulthood. His involvement within the family is critical and important to a successful family ties and family bonding.

Nowadays, more and more of mothers are in the workforce, thus the role of a fathers in the 21st century are demanding as ever. Dads taking huge responsibilities in household works, looking after the children and at times they can do it even better than their wives.

Fathers are expected to be the disciplinarians, but with kindness and softness in their hearts. Quite difficult to be achieved, however as always they can managed it efficiently and effectively.

All children when they were young enjoyed to be sitting on their father's shoulder. They felt tall and loved to see everything around them. This is what fathers do.

Father's love is unconditional. They will always be there for their children, but they do not condone wrong behaviour and attitude. They are firm in their decisions, yet always open to suggestions and ideas. They are willing to accept mistakes, these are the qualities of an ideal and a good father to his children

Father of a Bride, a movie made in 1991, typifies how a father can be overprotective to his daughter. The movie also exemplified how a father feels when his daughter decided to get married and start her own family. A comedy movie but I am sure fathers can relate to this.

An excerpt from my 2nd book
My Passion, My Calling

Through the eyes of the children
Their parents are their role models and heroes
Therefore it is the responsibility
Of every parent to set high standard
To be able to produce
Future responsible adults

6 Dad...The Hero

7
Love and Acceptance

Of human and divine love; which love is the greatest of them all, will you be able to sacrifice one for the other? Indeed a very sensitive and controversial topic. The answers will depend on your own perspective in life.

Whatever you choose, both of them have one thing in common – acceptance. Acceptance of responsibilities, commitments and sacrifices for the one you love.

The Cardinal, film of 1963 exemplified what divine love is. A young priest had to choose between the life of his sister and her unborn child. The head of the baby had to be crushed to save the mother, yet being a priest he did not allow this to happen, resulting in the death of the mother. That made him question his faith.

He requested a two year sabbatical leave and went to Vienna Austria to teach. There he met and fell in love with a girl, however the priest did not violate his vows of chastity and in the end he had chosen divine love. His love for God was stronger in his heart than human love.

Same heartaches and sorrow will be felt by a mother, who has no choice but to give up her newborn child for adoption for the sake of its welfare and future. Sacrifices have to be made for the sake of your loved ones.

Loving someone is not easy. You have to accept the whole package, his or her own imperfections.

Loving does not mean changing the person for your own personal intent. You will always feel pain and hurt whenever you see your loved one suffer. You will always worry about them.

But then again it's only a small price to pay for the joy and happiness that you feel, of loving and being loved.

Here is my unpublished poetry about love:

> Love encompasses everything
> Does not know boundaries
> It is so strong
> It will conquer all
> Along its path
> Does not care who you are
> Regardless of gender, status,
> Or beliefs.
> Makes a strong man cry
> And a weak man strong

8
Realities of Life

Just a simple, gentle squeeze on your hand from someone you love, can mean a thousand things. A wonderful token of love, affection, care, understanding, support and much more. It can be easily felt within your heart, a simple gesture, yet stronger and powerful, than any spoken words.

I do believe, it's not only saying "I love you," but it's all about caring and even doing sacrifices if needed for someone you love.

Love for me is the essence of what life is all about, happy are those who are surrounded with loved ones; faithful friends, and most of all loving families. These are the very people who will always be there for you regardless of what you are.

Of course it is not always easy for us to make choices, at times we falter along the way. People will despise, criticise, but you can still manage to be strong. You know there are those who believe in you. They are the reason for your inspiration to fight back until you can achieve your dreams and goals in life.

However there are those who are consumed by success, forgetting where they started. When everything had been taken away from them, they realised who their real friends are. They sought out the loving arms of their families.

We don't have to please everyone, there are people who won't appreciate you no matter what you do. Instead, concentrate more on those who love and care for you. They will always be there for you, thus making your journey easier and more meaningful.

You can read more of my inspirational messages from my two books. *My Innermost Thoughts* is a compilation of my poems, wisdoms, and beliefs. *My Passion My Calling* is a memoir, encompassing my journey as an author.

An excerpt from *My Innermost Thoughts*: "Why would I want all the wealth in the world? Why would I want all the fame and glory, where I don't know who are my real friends and enemies? Yes it's true, there are those who have both fame and glory, yet they don't have the peace within themselves. Out of desperation, their only way is to drown in drugs and alcohol, and then find themselves more confused, that will lead them to self-destruction and even death. I don't envy them. I think as long as I have enough to live, surrounded with people I love and trust. *I feel I am the luckiest person on earth.*"

9
What's in a Smile

A beautiful smile can melt anyone's heart, but what is really in a smile that inspires a poet to write, a musician to write songs about it, and Leonardo da Vinci to paint the Mona Lisa; the lady with a mysterious smile that captivates and fascinates all of us? Indeed do not underestimate the power of a smile.

How often do we meet and encounter strangers on the streets, shopping malls and indifferent places? Just a swift fleeting glance from them followed by a smile can mean a lot of things such as greetings; hello, how are you, wishing you the best of the day. A gesture that is more potent and powerful way of communicating other than words. The moment when you see loved ones, friends and relations, before uttering a word a smile from their faces say it all.

A smile is a symbol and image of our emotions and an expression of our inner self but nonetheless not all smiles are genuine and sincere. There are smiles that are deceiving, hurtful and insulting which is an ugly side of the human nature. There are those people who however, smile while hiding their frustration, sorrow and grief. They are the courageous ones who remain positive and continue to move on.

We always smile in front of the camera because we want to be remembered as happy contented people who enjoy that very moment when the photo is taken. Who can forget that beautiful smile from your first crush, your first love? A thrilling and exhilarating special moment that we had. Likewise, those gorgeous smiles from your children and your grandchildren will always be cherished in your heart.

When your children and grandchildren were small and were being naughty, a smile from their faces would stop me from being mad. But of course it would not deter me to explain to them the consequences of their actions. Every time we came home from a hard day's work at the office, a smile from the faces of our loved ones would always bring sunshine, joy and relief.

A smile can be infectious. If you are surrounded by people who are happy and smile, you feel comfortable and at ease, and at times you can alleviate your problems. Smiling can also have a tremendous effect on your health by lowering your stress level, hence leaving less negativity and a more positive outlook on life.

This is one of the best quotes from Mother Theresa, a recently canonised saint: "Every time you smile at someone, it is an action of love, a gift to that person, a beautiful thing." An awe inspiring and impressive quote that is always worth remembering.

You can do no wrong by smiling. It is good for the body and smiling symbolises contentment, peace and positive attitude. There is so much anger, negativity and chaos at present, and what the world needs now is smiling and happy people regardless of what the situation is. So keep on smiling and as the popular saying goes: "Smile and the world smiles at you, cry and you will cry alone."

Some original and unpublished quotes about smiles:

A smile can do wonder

It denotes friendship,

Peace and love

A beautiful smile coming from your loved one

Always brings inspiration and love

Especially when you are at the lowest ebb of your life

Just a simple smile

A warm hello

And a gracious thank you

Would make anyone's day

Very special

10
Spiritual Upliftment

Excerpt from
My Innermost Thoughts

If the food we take nourishes our body
Prayers, meditations and contemplation are the tools
For enriching and uplifting our spiritual souls
Through these we grow to control
Our minds and emotions
Thus bringing to the next level
Where inner peace and satisfaction can be achieved

We spend so much time, effort and money improving our bodies and physical appearances. Companies spent billions of dollars promoting products that claim eternal youth and beauty, but do we take time and effort to improve and nourish our souls? Do you see ads in the media or newspapers promoting the cleansing and purifying of our souls? I don't think so! It doesn't take too much of our time to say prayers, meditate, search for our souls, and yet we hardly do it. Why? Because we are more preoccupied with other worldly things and values such as the quest for glory fame and success. The desire to be the best in whatever we do, the desire to look attractive, punishing ourselves by doing extensive exercise to be fit and perfect.

Unfortunately I myself was a victim of these obsessions, but when I had gone through a critical point in my life it made me realise that everything was worthless. Everything that I had aspired for was no longer relevant, and what was more important was the purity of my soul, inner peace, and a strong connection with God.

Sometimes we do need to pause and question ourselves, ask "Is it all worth it?" All the hassles, pressure from work, keeping up with the modern trend, to be the best at what we do; denying ourselves of a much needed break and the special moments that are to be shared with our families and friends.

Saddened that there were people even in the last moments of their lives showed bitterness and discontent to everything around them and never found peace within. Nowadays most of us are more conscience of our image and our status in the community than being aware and mindful of our spiritual needs. Indeed, a sign of modern era.

By migrating to Australia we all have the same goal; to build a new life. There were some who had taken it to the extreme by working seven days a week or doing two jobs at a time. When their health was affected they wished they had spent and taken more of their precious time with their families. It was too late for them but luckily for others it was only a wakeup call.

Even with our children we pressure them to do well at school with our unrealistic expectation which drives them to be depressed and one of the many reasons for youth suicides. As parents we should be perceptive of our children's spiritual and moral developments, in the same way that we do for their academic performance. I believe there should be a balance to be able to produce happy, caring, more responsible adults once they have grown up.

Lastly something to reflect on; *we always mourn for the loss of loved ones and friends, but do we mourn for the loss of one's soul?*

11
The Art of Friendship

LOVE comes in many different forms, and one of them is in the form of *friendship*. A friend can be a mother, sister, or husband, but what I will be discussing in this article is the strong attraction within the interpersonal relationship between two people.

Since time immemorial, all of us have sought and pursued someone to trust, hence friendships blossom. Some friendships continue to exist from childhood up to the present that last forever; truly the best friendships to be desired.

There are times that we can only confide our darkest and innermost secret thoughts to our best friends, and not to our parents or loved ones. This is a token of reliance and loyalty that you are confident to share to your best friend. Friendship is unconditional, forgiving, and has a mutual understanding of each other. However, I strongly believe that in order for friendship to flourish and survive both should take responsibility to nurture it. To make an effort to negotiate what is fair for the interest of both sides.

Oftentimes we develop friendship with a person whom we share the same interests and beliefs. Different personalities can clash, but in rare cases friendships can also develop for two people who have different backgrounds and cultures. Likewise it can also be built based off compatibility either emotionally, spiritually, and psychologically.

A true friend will be able to tell you the truth - even if it hurts – with the intention to do what is best for you. A friend will always be there for you, especially during vulnerable moments in your life. Indeed it is a beautiful expression of friendship.

There are different levels of friendship, the first being your very best friend, and second, casual friends – the friends you associate with time to time and still consider to be a good friend. The third is a group of social friends who are bound together with the same objectives or goals, for example the friends that you have in different organisations doing the same activities or hobbies. The fourth kind are the internet friends such as Facebook friends, a sign of the modern technology of today.

Oftentimes I met with a group of friends who I have lunch with on a weekly basis. When we catch up with each other we share stories of whatever interests us. These are the friends that I have known for the decades since I came to Australia. With them is a day of laughter and jubilation.

One of the best examples of the true definition of what friendship is portrayed in the movie *Beaches*. Presumably most of us have seen this captivating story about two friends. Though they did have differences, her friend stood beside her and helped her go through her difficult times.

So what makes a best friend so special? Is it because you have the privilege of choosing a friend? Or is it because you know that your friend will always be there for you regardless. Whatever the reasons are, one thing is certain: friends will make us feel comfortable and important. They can bring out the best in us, and for me that is what friendships are all about.

An excerpt from
My Innermost Thoughts

Friendship
True friendship does not take
A day to make
It takes fine wine years to age
And to attain perfection
Friendship takes years to develop
Those memories good ones and bad ones
You share together
Accepting of ones faults
And indifferences
Understanding and forgiveness
And if time comes when you
Won't see each other again
Beautiful memories of friendship
That no one can take away from you
Will remain embedded
In your heart

12
The Many Faces of Happiness

An original unpublished poem

Happy are those who can forgive
Because they will find peace
Within themselves and others
Happy are those who stay connected with God
Because it is the only way to eternal salvation
Happy are those who are willing to share and help others
Because they make a difference in this troubled world we live in
And lastly happy are those who can love and accept people
Because they will be loved in return

Happiness will truly define who, what we are and what our priorities are in life. We go through different stages of happiness as we walk the journey of life. A small child will find happiness by playing with pots and pans or even by pulling tissues from a tissue box, ignoring expensive toys given by dotting parents. Expression of delight and joy on children's' faces when surrounded with candies, chocolates, cakes, and ice cream; those are simple gestures of happiness through the eyes of children.

As we grow older happiness becomes complicated. We set goals, achievements, and power. An ultimate happiness by many of us. For some people, there are those whose happiness can be achieved by sharing and helping others such as missionaries, community workers, soldiers, to name a few. They are special people who have talents that an "Almighty God" has provided them to share.

At the middle of our journey in life a different level of happiness is felt when we meet our soulmate or the love of our life, then becoming a parent. Sheer joy of happiness is experienced when we had our first born child. Our children are an extended version of ourselves, nurture them with love and they will do the same once they have families of their own. No greater happiness can be felt by parents knowing that their children lead a happy and successful life.

My own experience of happiness was that moment where I had the chance to hold my first born granddaughter. From the very first time that I laid eyes on her, I knew that I was blessed to be her grandmother. As I walk through life nearing the end of my journey, my happiness consists of looking after my grandchildren, being there for their first smile, first uttered words, and their first steps. It is an exuberant experience to be a grandmother, and I believe that all grandparents can relate to this.

As a guest speaker at one of the events that I attended I could feel the frustration and loneliness of the elderly. They felt left out and seeking for the attention, love, and care of their families. Fortunately in Australia, we have elderly organisations that are doing a fantastic job to help and entertain them with various activities that can alleviate their loneliness.

At the end we must remember that we will all grow old, and

when the time comes it's up to us to make our own lives interesting regardless of your age.

Akin to the happiness of a child, as we walk through the final journey our happiness becomes simple and uncomplicated. Indeed this is the cycle of life. As we grow older we also realise that *the simplest things in life are often the best.*

13
The Seasons of Life

There is something in the spring season that makes us sprightly and happy. Is it because of the anticipation of warmer days ahead, after the dreary cold winter? For me this is the reason why Spring is my favourite season of the year.

Spring symbolises new hope, new beginning, and new life. For an avid gardener who had done a lot of work fertilising, pruning, re-planting during Winter, this is the time for them to see the fruit of their labour. A bountiful leaves and flowers for the plants, the abundant product of the fruit bearing trees.

Through the window glass in my room I can see at my backyard, my Cherry, Plum, Apple, Peach, and Apricot trees, all showcasing their beautiful blossoms of white, pink, red colours. These blossoms will be turning into fruits at summertime for us to enjoy thus giving nourishment to our bodies.

The season of the year can be compared to our cycles of life. A new born baby resembles spring, symbolises new life, new hope, and will eventually reach its potential at its maturity. Same as the summer season where all plants, shrubs and roses will be at their peak of blooms displaying dazzling array of colours and flowers in all shapes and sizes.

Towards the Autumn season, leaves, flowers beginning to fall, ready for hibernation. For us this is the time for reassessing and reflecting things we had done. By the time Winter comes, some plants and trees will be dormant and for us we will be reaching the end of our journey. Then the whole cycle will start all over again.

Sometimes unexpected event or trauma will happen at any one stage of our lives. A friend of mine lost everything, the house, material possessions, irreplaceable memorabilia in a fire. Synonymous to Winter that is depressing, they managed to pull through. Their strong belief in "GOD" and the help of all their friends and religious congregation, alleviated their sorrows. They stay positive and instead count their blessings that no one lost their lives.

I am now in my twilight years, the Autumn season, slowly reaching the end of the journey. Looking back I am proud of what I had achieved; wonderful, law abiding successful children, well-mannered grandchildren, I am still interacting, connecting and sharing my thoughts and ideas through my writings to all people from all walks of life. If lucky hopefully I will have many more years of Winter seasons to enjoy.

My Unpublished Poem

Season Of Life
In every stage of life we had
In every Journey of life we tread
In every hardship and Pain
There will always be an end
Just like the winter cold and woeful
Spring will always follow alive and blissful

Forgetting the dark miserable wintery nights

14
'Tis' the Season to be Jolly

(3rd prize, Christmas Writing Competition by the Society Women Writers Victoria)

'Tis the season to be jolly fa-la-la-la…is the opening song from one of our favourite Christmas songs "Dec The Halls". This is a song filled with joyous moments and a picture perfect atmosphere of Christmas Season. For most of us this is true, especially through the eyes of children, anticipating opening lots of Christmas gifts. For adults, it is the season for endless parties, food gorging and alcohol consumption. For the privileged few, this is the time for luxurious holidays and cruises to exotic places. The Christmas time is also busy for religious group in the preparation in the commemoration of the birth of Christ.

To some people, Christmas do not have any significant importance, examples are; the sick, those without families and friends, people who are sufferings with mental problems or illnesses and the homeless.

For others, Christmas is a time of sorrow. Families who can not afford to give present to loved ones due to financial difficulty. For OFW (Overseas Filipino Workers), an agonising time for them celebrating Christmas away from loved ones. For the soldiers who are still in the battle zone serving their countries truly a miserable Christmas for them.

All shops will be decorated for this festive season, enticing

14 Tis' the Season to be Jolly

consumers to spend more, the sad part is we are falling to this trap of commercial propaganda thus forgetting the real essence of Christmas. The way we celebrate Christmas will depend in our perspective and lifestyle. There is no right or wrong, but one thing is certain, Christmas time will always bring special family bonding with loved ones and friends.

My first Christmas in Australia in 1977 was a memorable one. We were residing at the Maribyrnong Hostel and some Filipino migrant families who had been in Australia before us had organised a Christmas party for us. We had delicious Filipino dishes, a Santa Claus giving gifts to our children. This alleviate our loneliness of spending Christmas away from home.

Regardless of age, gender, belief or lifestyle I suppose that LOVE and for Christian community, the celebration of the birth of CHRIST are the main reasons of what CHRISTMAS is all about.

My unpublished reflective thoughts

God sometimes allowed us to have difficulties
In life
To suffer heartaches and sorrow
Not to punish us
But as a wake-up call
For us to realise we still need him
For Comfort and support
Hence making us a better
And stronger person than ever

15
Change and Humility

Welcoming the new year to come, most of us will try once again to make changes in our lives, embracing the year ahead full of enthusiasm and anticipation wishing the new year will be much better than the previous one. With changes we need a lot of perseverance and motivation in order to do it effectively.

Change and humility are two words that go hand in hand. I do believe humility is the aftermath of every change that we do. It is the acceptance and acknowledgement of one's faults and flaws and how can one improve to be a better and stronger person

Reassessing your inner self is the best way to start. Begin with the easiest part that is achievable then do it one step at a time until you reach your goal. How-ever all these entail discipline and determination. The ideal and perfect way to change is not only to benefit ourselves but also for the welfare and interest of others, especially our loved ones. Nonetheless there are those people who are not open other's opinions, hence humility is beyond their perception and grasp.

Certainly, change is inevitable, circumstances will change as we go to different stages of our lives. Indeed, it is a part of growing up and moving on. Then again it is up to us to determine if the change is feasible to avoid disappointment and frustrations.

A sinner who is asking for forgiveness truly embodies the whole concept of humility, accepting their imperfections and mistakes and surrendering their love to our God Almighty.

Lastly a very good and ultimate example of humility was shown by Jesus. Although He is the son of God. He gave His life to redeem us from sins. He accepted the path of humility, humbled Himself, obedient even to the point of dying on the cross

An excerpt from my book
My Innermost Thoughts

IMPERFECTION

That life does not need to be perfect
Imperfection, challenges, motivates, stimulates
The desire to grow and be a better person
Imperfection makes us humble
Helps us to accept things we can not change
Imperfection enables to see life
From a different perspective, and perhaps
We can see more in depth meaning of what life is all about

16
Planning To Retire?

Retirement is the most crucial stage in our lives. It is dreaded by some, while others look forward for it. Are you well equipped and prepared for this? There are people who are planning for their retirement in five years or even more, but some times it does not matter how prepared you are. There are some unforeseen circumstances that are beyond your control, such as health issues and death. One has to be flexible when these tragic events occur.

Readjustment is one of the key issues taken into consideration when retiring. Suddenly you are with your partner 24/7 hence it can be quite a shock to both of you. Unfortunately as a result of this, some couples divorce during this time. This is the time for reassessing, compromising, reconnecting with each other. I truly believe that if both people are still in love with each other this issue will be easily resolved.

Yes it is true that financial freedom helps in retirement. However quite a lot of people were not fortunate enough to amass wealth upon retirement. Do not despair, as long as you have your wealth, loving and caring families and friends and you are at peace with yourself and GOD, happiness is achievable. These are the things money can not buy.

We are fortunate here in Australia that there are many organisations that help elderly and retirees. They have monthly events, programs and entertainment. There are lots of ways to enjoy retirement such as socialising with friends and joining that you have interest in. This is the time to explore your hidden talents for example learning new hobbies such as painting photography, work volunteer, writing and for those who can afford it, travelling overseas or visiting beautiful places in Australia.

When I retired seven years ago, I had the privileged of looking after my grandchildren. It was the most exhilarating experience in my life. I also found my passion for writing and music. To date I had published two books and currently have a third book, a novel underway. I have returned to studying intermediate piano and have joined several organisations, started to socialise with friends that I have not otherwise seen in decades. So who said retiring is boring? Definitely not me.

An excerpt from
My Innermost Thoughts

I was often asked this question
Are you bored retired?
How do you fill up your time?
I just smile
Because I know within
I am enjoying every minute being retired
How can you be bored
Sharing every moment with your loved ones?
How can you be bored
Exploring and reinventing yourself?
How can you be bored doing things you are passionate about?
Absolutely my colourful life begins during retirement

16 Planning To Retire?

17
The Eyes Say It All

What words fail to say, the eyes say it all; a quote from my second book My Passion My Calling. Our eyes are the reflections and revelations of our inner self and emotions that no one can hide. What we say at times is different from what we really mean and our eyes can express it more effectively than any words spoken, hence true to the popular saying that our eyes are a window of our soul.

A pretentious and fake smile can easily be seen through the eyes of a person. People forget that their eyes reveal how they feel. The feelings of happiness and surprise cause our eyes to get bigger and to light up, than when the feelings are of sadness and loneliness.

" Look me in the eye if you are telling the truth" is a popular statement to determine is lying or hiding something. Nonetheless. There are different reasons why some people do not feel comfortable having eye contact. Culture, anxiety, distress, shyness or just "in love" are amongst the reasons for avoiding eye contact.

At times in both mankind and animal kingdom an eye contact can pose a threat or a challenge that can endanger one's life. I know of a good looking guy who had a glance at a group of people and they followed him and beat him.

Criminal Minds one of my favourite television shows had mentioned that the eyes of psychopath and criminals have one thing in common;

their intense gaze and their emotions are empty and dull. Their eyes appear to be very different than the norms. On a more romantic scale, an emotional and touching movie scene I had seen recently was at the end of the movie *La La Land*, whereby no words were spoken between the two main characters. Only through their eyes, at a gaze, they connected and understood what their hearts and souls are saying. A powerful way of demonstrating how our eyes can be stronger than words.

Here is an Excerpt from my book
My Innermost Thoughts

Others hide their sorrows
Through their smiles
Others hide their fears
Through acting fearlessly
Others hide their insecurity
By acting superior to everyone
At times the things we see
Are not really what they are
There are more depth and meanings
To consider before judging others

18
Love Conquers All

Just like the air we breathe that sustains our lives, yet we can not see it, love is something too intense to feel with our hears and souls but invisible to the human eye Love is the complete acceptance of someone who you care for and love, not who you want them to be. Love has no limits and it makes every moment of your life truly special. It is more potent than any lethal poison or venom known to man.

Love can divide nations and destroy families or friendship simply because it has no boundaries or rules to follow. Indeed it is quite difficult love as it is too complicated to fathom. It comes in many forms; the love of parents to their children, the divine love between people and GOD, the patriotic

One can not buy love, nor make someone love you, it can not be traded nor prevented. You can buy companionship, yet without love it is meaningless. Feeling in love is a surreal experience; you wont know when it will strike and at times it will catch you unprepared, akin to the saying "like a thief in the night". Hence it is the responsibility of both sides to be honest and trust worthy so that the relationship should be solid as a rock.

Love is freely given and should not be taken for granted by the recipient, so it will flourish and become stronger through the years

There is no such thing as a perfect marriage or relationship, but because of love for one another people will be able to resolve issues, or difficulties that can be detrimental to a relationship

Love is unconditional, forgiving, selfless, caring, inspiring but at times harmful and heartbreaking. I believe this is the highest form of human emotions. Almost all of us will choose love. A person without love and compassion within their hearts will never find the holy grail of happiness, contentment and the magical moments in life, that for me is not worth living for.

An Excerpt from my book
My Passion My Calling

Excuses will be made
Reason will be given
But
To show you care
And love someone
You do not need excuses
It should be manifested
In every way

19
Miracles Do Exist

An Excerpt from my book
My Innermost Thoughts

Who said miracles don't exist anymore?
From the moment I open my eyes each morning
I see the sun shining in the sky
Or hear the sound of the rain
Pouring down on my roof
I see life in it
Beautiful creations from GOD
Enjoying the sun
Feasting from the pouring rain
Crops that we planted
Bearing its fruit
I see miracle in this
Indeed, about the harmonious relationship
Of nature and mankind
A simple thing I can say
Is the miracle of life

Each breath we take and each time we wake up are already miracles.

19 Miracles Do Exist

Our body is the symbol of the miracle of life. Cells inside our bodies change consistently at all times. Different organs inside interact with each other, each one of them having different functions to give us continuous life on earth. I believe that this is a living proof of daily occurrences of miracles, something beyond our comprehension of the intricate structures of the human body.

The vast solar system and how it works, every planet collaborates with one another in a movement in a predictable way I called this a *miracle*. To the sceptics, doubters, and non- believers, they can always provide technical explanation for this. Needless to say for us Christians and other religions we strongly believe that there is a greater force beyond our grasp that is responsible for all these things to happen.

Is it just only an urban myth when we hear stories of people being cured after prayer or somebody being diagnosed with cancer and given only few months to live survive that leaves doctors baffled?

One of the most popular miracles had occurred on the 13th of October in 1917, in Fatima Portugal, witnessed by more than hundred thousand of people. It is the apparition of the Blessed Virgen Mary to the three shepherd children. According to many witnesses, after a period of rain, the dark cloud break and the sun appeared as an opaque spinning disk in the sky. It was well documented and the event was officially accepted as a miracle of the catholic church in October 13, 1930. How many times do we hear stories of babies and toddlers falling from a tall buildings and surviving? Would you consider this a miracle?

From my second book published in 2015 titled *My Passion My Calling* I described in the book the detailed story of my near-death experience and my first-hand encounter of the real essence of what a miracle was. After my recovery I developed a sudden passion in writing Inspirational Messages, a passion and desire that I did not have and feel before. I do believe I was given a second chance to live, to carry on a mission. To be able to help and reach people from all walks of life especially those who are confused, desperate and at their lowest ebb of their lives, through my inspirational writings.

This is the path that I have to follow and I am willing to do it as long as I am spiritually, physically and mentally capable. As I always say, sometimes a beautiful moment can happen and do not hesitate to follow it. Chase your dreams and most of all always chase your *destiny*.

20
Forgiveness as a Virtue

The lord's prayer, a prayer thought by Jesus to his disciples, is now recited by all Christians. A beautiful prayer very inspiring and a meaningful passage one of which is: Forgive us our trespasses as we forgive those who trespass against us"

How many times do we pray The Lord's Prayer? Do we really digest and comprehend the quintessence of its meaning especially the part about forgiveness. Forgiving those who betrayed us and the degree of harm inflicted on us is not easy, but with sheer determination it will be achievable.

By forgiving you can move on and have closure. If there is still hatred in your heart, inner peace can not be found, thus it will haunt you forever. People who forgive are happier, healthier and have a good positive outlook of life. They are prepared to start a new beginning and and the experiences they endured will serve as a lesson, making them stronger and able to face the future with confidence.

There are people who will choose revenge over forgiveness. One form of revenge is not hurting your opponents physically, but destroying them internally watching them fall apart emotionally, mentally and spiritually. Will you feel better doing this? I do not think so, you will be worse than ever and you will make the situation more complicated. As a saying goes *"a mistake can not be corrected by another mistake"*.

Lenten season is a holy celebration for Christians all over the world. It is a time for fasting and repentance, a time for reflection when Jesus died on the cross. His first of His seven last words spoken on the cross was " *Father forgive them for they do not know what they are doing*" Even up to the last hour of his death, He was talking about forgiveness. The second time He mentioned forgiveness was during the repentance of a sinner beside him. A paramount manifestation of the virtue of forgiveness. The world would be more peaceful, joyous and better place if forgiveness will always reign in our hearts.

An excerpt from my book
My Innermost Thoughts

Letting it go
Does not mean forgetting the past
It is merely a preparation
For a new beginning
For a new life, for a new hope
Use your past as an inspiration
For a better future

21
Journey of life

All of us have experienced different colourful stages in our lives, as we walk through the journey of life. Some are lucky to have a long journey of which they achieve fulfilment of their dreams, yet there are some who are unable to do so as they are taken by death prematurely.

At a very young age, the world, the world seems too big for our eyes. Everything around us is exciting and new to us. As we grow older our concepts of life change. The quest for knowledge becomes insatiable. We work hard for our ultimate desires, power and wealth. Then greed starts to slowly creep in and corrupts our body, mind and soul. But at the end of the journey we sometimes question ourselves: Is it all worth it?

At the prime time of our life, we think we are invincible, biting off more than we can chew. Keeping up with the modern times and keeping up with the joneses. But what really is a successful life? Is it measured by material possession or power? The answer will depend on your priorities in life. For me my priority is to have a relatively healthy body and a sound mind hence I can enjoy the rest of my journey.

Gaining experiences as we grow older makes us stronger, wiser and more compassionate. Why? Because our values change as we approach the end of our journey. What was relevant before is not now and is no longer important.

I had witnessed a very sad scenario that broke my heart. I was at the counter at a major grocery store and I overheard a son at his elderly mom: the mother had picked up the wrong item. In a soft tone of voice, she was telling her son that she could go back and change it. But the son angrily told her that he did not have time to wait for her.

Will this happen to me, will my loved ones treat me like this if I am no longer productive and strong? Scary thoughts indeed. Nonetheless, there are quite a lot of heart-warming scenarios; I had seen sons and daughters caring and looking after their elderly parents even bringing them to festivities and events, thus taking the time to share precious moments together. These will always put a smile on my face. I do hope my love ones will do the same for me and would never forget me in my old age…….. Well time will tell

Journey of Life

In our younger days we were so eager
To learn new things, venture new experiences
Enjoy each time we went through
Extensive knowledge, we so desires
BUT,
It is in our mature years we can comprehend
Understand, appreciate
Appreciate everything we learned
And all the experiences as we
Walk through the Journey of life

21 Journey of life

22
Mothers, The Most Loved People On Earth

I believe our life's journey starts in our mother's womb. Mothers giving us all the nourishment needed making us stronger by the day. After nine months, a mother will give the most precious gift to the world: a new born child.

The cutting of the umbilical signifies the physical separation of a mother and a child. However the connection and bonding continues. The baby still needs nourishment from the first day he/she was born with the mother giving breast milk to her baby. Indeed the child can feel a mother's first touch hugs and kisses and the warm caring love she gives.

The profound love of a mother to her children can never be fathomed. It defies logic and reasonable explanations. An example of unconditional love, a love that is full of sacrifices and caring.

Its not only human who manifested our love for our offspring, but also to the animal kingdom. One documentary I saw on TV, a scene that really touches my heart, showed a big cat protecting her new born from predators, diverting the attention from her newborn resulting in herself becoming a victim or a casualty. A pinnacle example of what a mother's love is.

A face that only a mother can love is an expression. A saying that epitomises the overall description of a mother's love to her children.

There is a strong connection of love, trust, and intensity between a child and their mother. The influence of a mother to her children is very significant in the process of their development. As shown by the overwhelming scientific and psychological studies. Children that are well loved are mostly self-confident, happy and have a good positive outlook on life.

So let us not celebrate Mother's Day only once a year, but everyday as a recognition of their role in moulding, loving and all the sacrifices they do for their children.

An excerpt from my book
My Passion My Calling

A Mother's Heart

A mother's heart is so strong
It can withstand all the pain
Sorrows and heartaches

A mother's heart will always
Forgive
No matter what
A mother's love will always give
Even if there is no more left to give
One can not fathom a heart
Of a mother
Unless you are a mother

23
Thanks for the Memories

Each year will come and go, and at the end of each year we are always in the process of preparing, assessing and evaluating the things we had done and had happened in our lives. There are memories that can be forgotten but there are some that can linger on forever and will always make us happy.

Both pleasant and painful memories can happen for the past year, and for the unfortunate ones, this is the time to move on and try to embrace the coming year with hope, new life and a new beginning. From the past mistakes we can now set up new goals and aspirations. For grieving families who lost loved ones, remember to concentrate for the living loved ones who still need your care and support.

It is no use having a long list of New Year's resolution. Based from statistic only 8% people will keep their New Year's resolution. Nonetheless remember that the choices we made will create and shape our future.

Be practical and sensible when making a resolution, start with the easiest one, take baby step and when you feel you are ready you can set or aim for your next goal. By doing this it won't create disappointment and frustrations.

Prioritise what is important, but consider as well that your changes will benefit not only yourself but your loved ones. Ask you family for support if needed and I am sure they will always be there for you.

I am truly thankful for the memories for the past year. It was the year that we celebrated our 50th wedding anniversary, the same year I had launched my 3rd book and my first novel "Moments of Love, Lust and Ecstasy. The previous year I decided to continue my piano study and fortunate enough to pass the Australian Music Examination Board for intermediate level.

This time I won't be making any New Year's Resolution instead I will continue my passion for writing, music and supporting my Charity.

Thanks for the outgoing years for all the wonderful memories I had and I hope next year ahead will be the same or better for me and for all of us.

Excerpt from my book
My Innermost Thoughts

It is the choice we make in our lives
That makes life itself
Full of challenges and surprises
Hence shaping and creating
Our journey of life

23 Thanks for the Memories

24
Divine Intervention

There are so many things in our lives that can happen without logical explanations. For sure atheist and non-believers will always have their doubts. They will have technical explanations then hide their frustrations once they run out of reasons. " A *blip or glitch of the system*" will be used as their explanation. They refused to accept that miracles do exist. I do believe in miracles and a Divine Intervention.

What is really a Divine Intervention? According to Google, it is a miracle or an act of God that causes something good to happen or stop something bad happening.

I am no stranger to this kind of phenomenon, and will gladly share my eerie experienced we had last New Year's-eve in 2017. My landline was not working for the last three months. I can call but we can not receive incoming calls. We were about to leave at 5:30 pm going to the city and the phone rings. At long last the phone was working again. It was a call from a friend inviting us to celebrate and welcome the coming year at their house. I told her to hang up and call again. This time it did not work. Requested few friends to call us but with negative results.

We visited our loved ones in the city, spent precious time bonding with them then we left around 10:30 pm to go to my friend's house to welcome the coming year with full of hope for a better year to come. So much enjoyed the party that it was already 2:30 am when we decided to go home. As we opened the door the house was fully lighted, ransacked and like a war zone. The robbers entered the back door of the laundry room. , and a bolo Machete from the laundry was taken and could be used to hurt or even killed both of us. Valuables, computers, designer bags etc were taken. Material things can be replaced, and it was a blessing we were not hurt.

Both of us were traumatised about the incident. We were lucky we were not at home when the home invasion happened. Just one phone call from a phone that was defective saves our lives. My new phone provider cannot give technical explanation why I was able to receive an incoming call that afternoon. He said: Probably a glitch in the system.

I do not think so. I personally think this is one good example of a Divine Intervention. I was given again a third chance of life. My second chance of life was fully discussed in detailed from my second book *My Passion My Calling*. Being angry with them will not change what had happened. I feel sorry for their lost souls and I pray may they find the right path of direction to follow.

Because of this incident it gave me an unequivocal assurance of strength, confidence to follow "HIS" calling; that is; to continue and fulfil my mission of promoting: Love, Peace, Compassion through my books and written articles and I will continue doing this, with the best that I can offer.

An excerpt from my book
My Passion My calling

Once we had gone through trials and tribulations
The more we appreciate the real essence
Of what life is all about.
It is not just living our lives
But it is all about how we live
Our lives on earth

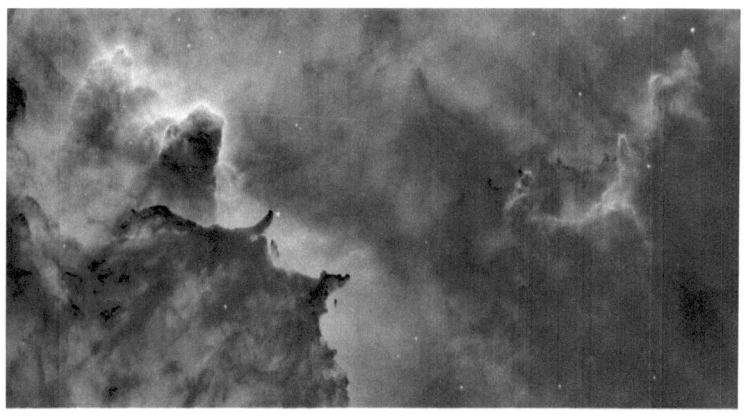

B.
Reflections

A.
Poems

1. **SEASONS OF LIFE**

    In every stage in life we had
    In every journey and experience we had
    For every hardship, sorrow and pain
    There will always be an end
    Just like the winter cold and woeful
    Spring will always follow
    Alive and blissful
    Forgetting the dark, miserable winter nights
    And moving to a bright new life
    For a fresh beginning and a new way of life

2. **FINDING LOVE**

    Being in love we start
    To rediscover our inner- self
    And the real meaning of what
    Life is all about
    Finding love is magical
    Moments and precious time
    We shared with someone
    We truly love and adore
    Finding Love is priceless

3. **HAPPINESS**

Happy are those who can forgive
Because they will find peace
Within and others
Happy are those who stay - connected
With HIM
It's the only way to eternal - salvation
Happy are those who are willing to share
And help others
Because they can make a difference
In this troubled -world
We live in
Happy are those who can love
And accept people
Because they will be able to love and be loved

4. **A SONG OF LOVE**

I cannot count the number
Of the stars in the sky
But I can see its brightness
Beauty and grandeur
I cannot fathom the depth
Of the deep blue sea
But I can feel its serenity
Calmness and tranquillity
It's the same as
I cannot tell you
How much I love you

But I can feel within my heart
The depth and intensity
Of my love for you

5. **MY ORDEAL**

So much pain and sorrow I feel
Akin to a sword or dagger
Slowly piercing through my heart
Dissecting it to pieces
At times I thought
I died a thousand times
Then each time bouncing back to life
Fighting as hard as I can
Wishing to overcome all these
Please help me God

6. **THE POWER OF LOVE**

Love encompasses everything
Does not know its boundaries
It is so strong and powerful
It will conquer everything
Along its path
Does not care who you are
Regardless of gender, status or beliefs
Makes a strong man cries
And a weak man strong

7. **ABOUT LIFE**

   One should to know when to stop
   One should know to call it quits
   But then again
   One should know when to start
   All over again
   Timing plus luck are an important roles
   In doing it efficiently and effectively

8. **DECEIT AND HONESTY**

   Deceit and honesty are always with us
   Since time immemorial
   These are the reasons
   Why we have conflicts
   Amongst Nations and people
   Indeed- a harsh realities of life
   All of us can make a difference
   If we start to practice the virtue
   Of compassion, love and tolerance
   For one another

9. **ETERNAL FLAME**

   One of the sweetest things in life
   Is to be able to share moments
   With your love ones up to the
   Last journey of your life
   To be able to look back together
   Those beautiful and unforgettable memories

To be able to grow old together
Learning to accept each -others
Faults and shortcomings
To be able to let the flame of love
We always cherish be
Forever in our hearts
Will remain as passionate forever.

10. **THE FOUNTAIN OF YOUTH**

Most of us are always seeking
The fountain of youth
Yet our spiritual nourishment
Seems to be for-granted
Everybody wants power and fame
Yet few people are fighting for a cause
Fighting for the oppress
Few are taking actions and solutions
For all- the humanitarian problems
We do face globally

11. **THE POWER OF MUSIC**

Such mystical, magical influence
In anyone's life
It eases, changes and affect
Our emotions and moods
Does alleviate and relieve
Whatever sorrows, heartaches we have
At times bring back beautiful

Memories of past years gone by
Thanks for the musician, composers, and singers
Who bring colours to our lives
Through the majestic moving sound of MUSIC

B. Inspirational Thoughts and Messages

1

People always love the underdogs
They will always sympathise for them
A good quality of us
However — once the underdogs bounce back
Thrive in their new-found success and fame
    Surpassing sympathisers
That's the start of bigotry, indifferences and conflicts

2

It is easier to understand rocket science
Than the complexity and intricacy
Of human minds, thoughts and emotions

3

Pain and hurt will be needed
To make us humble, a wake- up call
Realising that
We still need HIM for strength and support

4
God sometimes allowed us
To have difficulties in life
Not to punish us
But to remind us
We still need Him
Hence making us a better
And stronger person than ever.

5
We came to this earth alone
Through our journey
We were able to create happy families
Beautiful friendship and memories
At the end we leave the world alone

6
The illusion that we created
At times brings joy
Or heartfelt anguish and sorrow
Especially when the expectations
And the realisations, that all things
Will -come to an end.

7

We tend to be a prisoner of our own self

Remembering past experiences

Too scared to move on

To let it go

Conquering with fear one's

Mind and soul

We always blame others, destiny and fate

Giving excuses for our failures

Failing to accept our own inadequacies

8

The season of Winter is akin to the darkest moments of our lives

Unforeseen - traumatic tragedies will happen

As long you have a solid faith in God

And the support of loved ones and friends

You can overcome all your predicaments.

Soon Spring will be around

New hope, new beginning

Our journey will be rosier and joyful

Than ever

9

Whatever we do

Whatever the outcome will be

If we did it with

Dignity and passion

That's all that matters

Its- only a start of a challenge

Let all our experiences be our guide

And all the things we learned

From our journey

With the right focus and determinations

Success is within our reach

10

Once you conquer your fear

There is no turning back

The only way is to move forward

Then the smell of success

Is imminent and reachable

11

At times out of desperation we do things

Hurting not only ourselves

But people around us

Loved ones, friends and families

They are the people you will need for support

And strength

12

Once or few times in our lives
We made crucial decision
That can change the path
Of our life's journey
This is challenge, without it
You cannot improve and
Dreams will be unreachable

13

Truth hurts but one should have
The courage to face it
In- order to move on
Tomorrow will be brighter than
The past and the present

14

Yes, we do receive all the blessings
    From HIM
But are we willing to share all these
    To the less fortunate?

15

It is in our own weakness that
We desperately tried to hide
Yet we easily judge others
Their imperfections and shortcomings

16

We will be able to improve and, analyse
Our own imperfections
By knowing the imperfections
And mistakes of others

17

The art of listening has a lot of advantages
You will be able to analyse
And read between the lines
What people are trying to hide or convey
An effective way of getting through
Their inner thoughts

18

If each one of us will do an act
Of kindness even once in your life
The world will be a perfect place
To live

19

Envy is akin to a poison
Creeping our body
Slowly polluting our mind body and soul
Saddest part is the person is not even aware of it

20

In time of troubles and tribulations
We seek and remember "HIM'
Do we still connect, and pray to "HIM"
In time of abundance and glorious
Joyful moments?

21

I believe each one of us has a mission
   On Earth
To follow "HIS" teachings
To use our talent bestowed to us
In the best possible ways
To help; share, and serve others
There are those who use their talents
For greed, power and - eventually
Will end up to their own
Self- Destruction

22

Life is full of surprises and regardless
Of what they are we should always
Be prepared and flexible
And be able to cope everything
That cross our path
Lucky are those who have support
From families and friends
But think of those
Who got no one to turn to

23

Deep within you know you had not changed
It's the people around you had
Sometimes it does hurt that old friends
Though not all of them, failed to support you
New found friends are the ones who did.
Do not be disappointed. Continue achieving
Your goals in life. Always remember do not expect
To please everyone. Look after yourself first
No one will do it for you

24

There are people who will give
More than they have
While they are those
Who will get more than
They should

25

I do believe that the character of a person
Will be greatly manifested
On how they treat another person
Regardless of their status in the community
And for what - they can do for you

26

Lucky are those people who were given
    A second chance
To rectify their mistakes
To be able to change their journey
    Of life

27

Age should not be a barrier
In chasing and following one's dreams
It is the passion in our hearts
That will make us truly alive
And looking forward for tomorrow's blissful
Journey and challenges

28

The more you had experienced
Heartaches and sorrows
The more you can transcend effectively
Your thoughts, ideas and emotions
In your writings

29

No one should ever sacrifice
Their happiness, because of the
Pressure from society, friends
Or even families

30
There is no need to run away
From something that is important
And matters to you
Just to please others
Always remember to follow
Your heart - that will lead you
To the right direction

31
Sometimes and most of the time
The anticipations are more agonising
Than the actual results
Or event that will happen

32
You would think that your life
    Is perfect
Till one day there are things
Happened beyond your control
Whatever they are we have
To learn to accept it
Just count your blessings for
All the things you still have

33

In love we rediscover

Our inner self

And the real meaning of

What life is all about

Love teaches us to be humble

Love teaches us to be forgiving

To be sensitive and compassionate

34

Often you will realise your priceless

Possessions are the least

Expensive ones

Enjoy and make the most of

What you have

Than complain of what

You do not have

....35

Always treasure and cherish

The company of loved ones

And friends while you still can

36

Let no hate, greed and jealousy

Reign in our hearts

Or you will not find peace forever

37

Make each day a celebration
    Of Life
A life full of hope
A life full of positive attitude
Negativity will always
Produce stress and unhealthy
For the mind and soul

38

It is not enough to say the word
    "I Love You"
To your loved ones
It must be be manifested by actions
Or else the words will be meaningless

39

If Passion becomes an obsession
Followed by greed. It will turn a person
To a monster. He will destroy everything
Along the way
No matter what would be the consequences

40

People will always forget what you say
People will never forget
How you treat them
And how you make them feel

41

The saddest part of one's life
Is living without love
Alienated with others
They are too busy working success, wealth
    And fame
At the end it is too late, finding themselves
Alone and miserable
    Is it worth it?

42

People around you and the
Environment you grew up
Will have a great influence and impact
It will shape what you will
Likely to be in the future

43

Always be happy and do not worry
Too much about what others will say
Follow your heart
Avoid negativity
Think positive and you will get
Positive results

44

The sacrifices we do for our children
To give them a better future
Will be always our priority
Though we are not expecting
Anything in return
It is still nice to be acknowledged
By them for everything we did.

45

Music   Heals the souls
    So Powerful
It somehow affects us
In so many different
    Ways

46

It is not about what you want to be
It is all about What you are meant to be
That's when Destiny takes full control

47

However intense the pain
    We felt
Grieving for the death of loved ones
We should to remember, we are only
Temporary residence on this world
Life should go on until the day
It is our turn to leave
And will come face to face
With our creator

48

Denial is your utmost enemy and hindrance
For your success, progress and growth
Though it is quite difficult to change
Do one step at a time
Until you succeed

49

When the music stops
And the laughter had vanished
That is the time you will realised
And know who your real friends are

50

Being open minded about
Everything in life is quite
Brain stimulating
You become more tolerance
Accommodating and non-judgemental
And be able to relate to everyone

51

We are all different That makes life interesting
Just imagine if we are all the same
Life will be very boring

52

It will be impossible to change a person
At least what we can do is
To give them something
To think about

53

It takes a person with integrity and honesty
To say I am sorry. While it takes a fool and
Self – centred person to deny
And accept
Their mistakes

54

Nowadays we are more conscious
Of our physical Image than
Our spiritual needs
A sign of the modern times

55

So sad there are people even at the
Last moments of their lives
Still show bitterness, discontentment
Hence   peace -within themselves
And others were never achieved

56

The beauty of nature never ceases to amaze me
Who said Miracles do not exist anymore?
Just look around you
And you will find the answers

57

One should not stop improving thyself
Regardless of age, gender
This what makes life more interesting
And more reasons and inspirations
To live

58

We keep on searching endlessly
But at the end we soon realised
The most prized possessions are the
Least expensive ones and at times for free

59

Anyone can do the things their heart desires
It is just a matter of sheer perseverance
Hard - work and the determination
To make it happen

60

We need to stop and question ourselves
Is it all worth it?
All the hassles, pressure from work
Keeping up with modern times
To be the best of the things we do
Denying ourselves with the - needed break
To spend special - moments with the loved ones
Friends? At the end you will realised
You can not bring back those wasted years
It is too late. You ended up miserable and
Discontented as ever.

61

There will be moment in our lives that we
Had reached our lowest ebb. The support
Of our families and friends are the only
Way to keep us going, giving us strength
To face life challenges and above all
Our faith in "Him" will give us the hope
We so desire.

62

Quest for knowledge is never ending
The desire for adventure, calculated risks
Are amongst the spices of life

63

Being aware always of what is going on around you
Being focused will give you the edge
To be upfront from your competitors
Truly a recipe for success for all
Professionals and entrepreneurs

64

It does not take too much effort
To do an act of kindness
Yet there are people who chose
To inflict pain and misery to others

65

A smile can do wonders
It can mean a lot of things
It denotes friendship peace
Appreciation and kindness

66

Appreciate even the smallest things
Of what you have
Enjoy all your blessings day by day
Always hope that the best things
In your life still will come
Staying positive is the way to live

67

Controlled risk is much better
Than not taking risk at all
One way you can achieve success

68

Love, Understanding, compassion
Are three beautiful traits
You can give to all fellowmen

69

Pretending to be what you are not
Will not get you anywhere
It will only add on to your frustrations

And at the end It will complicate

Your life and deepens your insecurity

70

You do not have to prove anything

To anyone. You are what you are

They should accept you as you are

And not what they want you to be

71

Accepting criticism is the way

You can evaluate, improve

And re assessing oneself

72

It is how you perceive life

That can make or unmake a person

The choices we made can shape

Our future and the path of the journey

Of your life you want to follow

73

Each one of us is special

That is how "HE" created us

It is up for us to find it

To believe in our self

Continue searching and following

Your dreams

74

Beautiful expression of oneself
One's emotions and powerful lyrics
Soul moving melodies
Can be felt by all of us
Through the magical sound of music

75

We always do not appreciate
Things we already have
We keep on searching and searching
For the holy grail of happiness
Until one day we realised
It is already within us all the time

76

Angels do not need wings
You can be an angel
By reaching and help others
Each one of us can make a difference

77

Let not grieving overtake your mind
Body and soul. Connecting with HIM
Through prayers and meditation
Can ease the pain you feel
Remember there are people
Who still love and care for you

78

I wonder what will be my life
Without the love of families and friends
My soul will be empty Then living
Will be miserable and lonely

79

It is the thought of a permanent or temporary
Separations from our loved ones
Can make us feel unhappy or grieving
Hence creating a big impact in our lives
And at times permanent hole in our hearts
That will take many years to mend
And sometimes it will never heal

80

I do believe, no matter what you become
Do not forget your root
Where you came from
    AND
The people who helped you
Become of what you are today

81

Few times in my life
That I got frustrated
Because things did not happen
    My Way
And I started to question
Why me?
At the end I realised that it had to happen
For my own benefit
I do believe for every predicament encountered
There will always be a silver lining ahead

82

At the twilight years of our lives
We realised that these are the most
Important factors in life:
    Health
    Inner peace
    Families and friends
    Food and shelter
All the rest will only be secondary

83

All actions are done with intentions
And motivations
Quite a few times we failed to recognise
Analyse and understand the aftermath of it.

84

Those who suffered the most
Will know and appreciate
The value and the real essence
Of what happiness is all about.

85

Power and greed when combined
Will be so lethal and addictive
Akin to the most dangerous drugs and substance
Known to mankind
The havoc they will produce
Will be mind- blowing

86

I feel closer to my Creator
Each time I am in my garden
Digging the soil, planting trees and flowers
Or just admiring the beauty of nature
Whenever or wherever I maybe

87

At times we do not allow
Love, understanding and compassion
Reign and flourish in our hearts
Because we are focus on ourselves
And let greed and hunger for power
Prevail within

88

It is not about being passionate
On what you believe
It is all about doing what
You believe into actions

89

Regardless of what had happened
Regardless of what reasons they are
One must face life with courage
Continue to move on
Just for the sake of all the people
Who still love and care for you

90

Maturity begins when you start
To accept and respect people
As they are and not what you
Want them to be

91

When love grows
Amidst all the hatred and chaos
It becomes more powerful
Intense and meaningful

92

Love will always find
And makes its way
No matter when where
And how

93

You shall never presume
You are the best
Because someone, somewhere
Will be better than you

94

The hurt is more intense
    And painful
When it comes from someone
You love, trusted and cared for

95

One's life experiences
Enhances your knowledge
Strengthen one's character
And served one's guiding light
As one's walk through
The journey of life

96

Who are we to judge others
Where our own imperfections
We just ignore and do nothing
About it

97

There is nothing more gratifying
Than to see your family
Eating with gusto
From the labour of love
Of the food you cooked
And prepared for them

98

Regardless of what people will say
Regardless of what people will think
    About you
If you really believe in what you do
You should go on and push through
These are only one of the many things
You will encounter
In achieving your dreams

99

I believe the real and true happiness
Can only be achieved
By sharing special moments
With loved ones, families and friends

100

Time is the master of our lives
Brutal unforgiving, relentless
Waste it
Then suffer the consequences
Time can never be taken back
Nor can be retrieved

101

No matter how fast you run
Darkness will always follow you
You got the choice confronting
Your demon
Or forever be a prisoner of yourself
And peace within can never be found

102

There will always be a thin line
Between obsession and passion
Once it starts to frustrate you
And the continuous craving
For the ultimate desire for success and fame
That is where obsession is taking over your passion
Hence it will create detrimental consequences
On your values, spiritually and morally
It will change the way you perceive life

103

Simple lessons in life:
It is always best to have moments of evaluation
Assessment and recollection of the
Things happening in your life
Do make priorities of what is important
Concentrate more on people
Who care, love and support you
Who will be there for you
Regardless of the situation
Disconnect to those who don't
Do not be affected with criticism
Instead use them for your own advantage
Hence making you a better and stronger person

104

True love lingers on
Even up to the last breath of your life
All sacrifices will turn into glory
Just for the sake of the people
You adore and love

105

Though at times expectation
Can bring heartaches and pain
Without it
We do not have the motivation and inspiration
To follow and chase your dreams

106

It is not only saying
In words you love someone
But it is all about caring and even
Sacrificing if needed
For someone you are deeply in love

107

One cannot fully appreciate
The sweet glory of success
Until you gone through failures
Trials and hardship along the way
One can- not achieve peace happiness
And serenity in life
If greed, envy and jealousy
Existed in your heart
One can -not fully fathom
The joy of living
Until you open your heart
Giving yourself a chance
To love and be loved

108

Growing up to an adult
Does not mean
You are invulnerable
To all evils that always
Existed in this world

109

Wondering what tomorrow will bring?
I just go on moving forward
Till I will reach my goal
Till success will be achieve
That is what life is all about

110

Just one moment that had happened
    In your life
Your perspective in life
Will have a complete turnaround
Change will be inevitable
Past dreams won't be feasible
You start to think of different
Alternatives in the future

Also by Lorna Ramirez

Lorna Ramirez wrote this book so she could share her wisdoms with others. She has been an observer of human behaviour and emotions and has built up her own personal philosophies throughout her life. This book is a collection of her strong beliefs and convictions and offers encouragement and enlightenment to others who may be lost and confused or be looking for some positive advice and assistance. Lorna Ramirez is a woman of strong beliefs in her faith and advocates believing in oneself, perseverance when times are difficult and living in the present.

These original poems and wise sayings will be enjoyed by readers young and old, from any walks of life, for their simplicity and beauty.

This authentic story about a Filipino migrant family settling in Melbourne in 1977 is a fascinating read, as it tells of the emotions, the ups and downs, the government assistance in those days, the practicalities, the difficulties, the sudden change of lifestyle and culture but also the joys of living in Australia in the 1970s, a 'paradise' in so many ways, with great opportunities for a good life.

The wife suddenly is confronted with severe trauma, closely followed by another, a time in their lives when everything appeared perfect. Her near death experience results in new beliefs and understanding and inspires her to write.

After a traumatic experience at the hands of four men, Eliza Martinez leaves her family and home in the Philippines to find happiness in Australia. But tragedy happens again in her life. Again she must overcome all predicaments in order to pull through and move on.

As a twist of fate makes her a victim of love, she realises the importance of having support during her journey through life. She comes to rely on her friends and family — even as she considers what it would mean to start a family of her own.

This is a story of romance, forbidden love and courage; a story of human sufferings, vulnerability and how the choices we make change our lives.

www.ingramcontent.com/pod-product-compliance
Lightning Source LLC
Chambersburg PA
CBHW031424290426
44110CB00011B/507